To My Grandchild,

_____

With love from,

_____

Date

_____

*For the L*ORD *is good; His mercy is everlasting,*
and His truth endures to all generations.

PSALM 100:5

ISBN 0-8499-5911-X

Printed in the United States of America
05 06 07 08 RRD 29 28 27 26 25

Grandmother's Memories

TO HER GRANDCHILD

Featuring the art of THOMAS KINKADE

Written by Candy Paull

Tommy
NELSON

Thomas Nelson, Inc.
Nashville

To the Reader:

One of the most important lifelong friendships you can develop is with your grandmother, and the best way to do that is by building memories. Surprisingly, it is the simple things that you are likely to remember most—listening to family stories over a plate of brownies, picking blueberries together, attending church. Time spent with a grandmother is time spent with someone who treasures you for who you are, who sees your potential and encourages your dreams.

Growing up, I did not have the opportunity to see my grandparents as much as I would have liked. I do remember that one of my grandmothers was a great big, tall, heavy-set Irish-German woman. She had been a fry cook on the railway lines, and that was one of the ways she had made money to help the family during the Depression and afterward. She had a commanding presence, and when my grandmother asked you to do something, you did it! Yet, she was also very whimsical and funny—she was always pulling little surprises on us. And, she lived just a few miles from Disneyland!

I look back with fondness on the few memories that I have of my grandparents. I wish that as a child I could have known that the time I would have with my grandparents would be very limited, and that I should enjoy every moment.

Your grandmother must love you very much. It takes a lot of time and thought to complete this journal, to share stories and family history and dreams. I imagine that if you read these pages carefully, you will find that not only is your grandmother a fascinating person, but you may be more like her than you think.

In Psalm 78:1–4, the Bible says,

> *My people, listen to my teaching. Listen to what I say. I will speak using stories. I will tell things that have been secret since long ago. We have heard them and know them. Our fathers told them to us. We will not keep them from our children. We will tell those who come later about the praises of the LORD. We will tell about His power and the miracles He has done.* (ICB)

This is what your grandmother has done for you with this journal. It is my hope that the words and paintings in this journal bring you closer to your grandmother and to our Heavenly Father.

Dearest Grandchild,

This journal is my gift to you. I have filled it with my love, my memories, and my dreams for the future. I have written in these pages about the things I once did and the things I learned. And I have written here about the person I am now and the things I consider most important in life. I hope this helps you understand who I am.

Your heritage is rich with the love of God and family, and it is this legacy of faith

that I wish to pass on to you.

I love being your grandmother. One of my sweetest memories is of the first time

I held you in my arms. I thank God every day for you and pray that this journal will

be a keepsake to remind you always of how much your grandmother loves you.

Always,

_____

*Now faith is the substance
of things hoped for, the
evidence of things not seen.*

HEBREWS 11:1

MY BIRTH

My full maiden name

I was given this name because

My birth date and place of birth

So teach us to number our days,
that we may gain a heart of wisdom.

PSALM 90:12

What was happening in the world when I was born

My mother's full maiden name

Her birth date and place of birth

My mother's best story about growing up

One of my most precious memories of my mother

Her children rise up and call her blessed;
her husband also, and he praises her.

PROVERBS 31:28

ABOUT MY FATHER,
Your Great-Grandfather

My father's full name

His birth date and place of birth

My father's best story about growing up

And he will turn the hearts of the fathers to the children,
and the hearts of the children to their fathers.

MALACHI 4:6

One of my most precious memories of my father

MY FAMILY

My brother's and sister's names

_____

_____

The things we used to do together

_____

_____

_____

_____

_____

The things we do together now

_____

_____

_____

_____

_____

How often I see my family

_____

_____

_____

Therefore comfort each other and edify one another,
just as you also are doing.

1 THESSALONIANS 5:11

I have seen God work in our family by

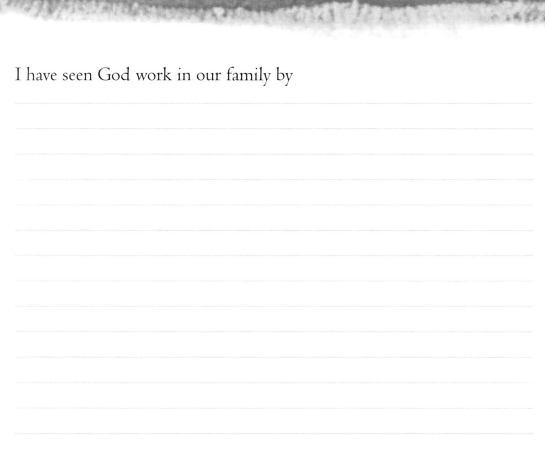

MY CHILDHOOD HOME

My earliest memory of home

_____

_____

_____

_____

_____

My childhood bedroom

_____

_____

_____

_____

My favorite hiding place

The yard I played in

For we know that if our earthly house, this tent,
is destroyed, we have a building from God, a house
not made with hands, eternal in the heavens.

2 CORINTHIANS 5:1

MY HOMETOWN

The street I lived on

_____

_____

_____

_____

_____

Where I played with my friends

_____

_____

_____

_____

_____

My favorite store and why I loved to go there

_____

_____

_____

_____

_____

_____

And there was great joy in that city.

ACTS 8:8

Where we worshiped

A TYPICAL DAY GROWING UP

Where my father worked

_____
_____
_____
_____
_____

What my mother did during the day

_____
_____
_____
_____
_____

The chores I had to do

_____
_____
_____
_____
_____

Blessed are the pure in heart, for they shall see God.

MATTHEW 5:8

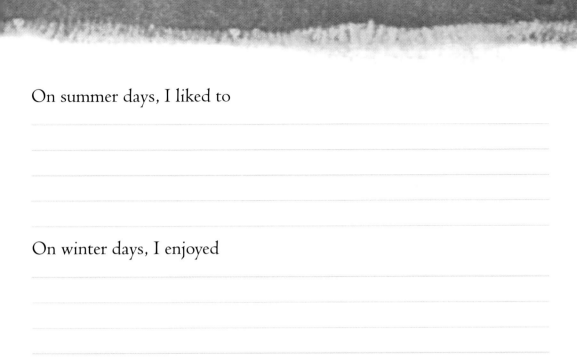

On summer days, I liked to

On winter days, I enjoyed

CHILDHOOD FAVORITES

My favorite storybook

My favorite poem

My favorite doll or toy

My favorite games

My favorite treat

My cup runs over.

PSALM 23:5

MY PETS

My first pet

My favorite pet

The different kinds of pets I have owned

*Out of the ground the LORD God formed every beast
of the field and every bird of the air, and brought them
to Adam to see what he would call them.*

GENESIS 2:19

Some of my pets' names

I always wanted a

WHEN I WAS A LITTLE GIRL

What an ice cream cone cost when I was young

What an ice cream cone costs today

The kind of car we drove

How people dressed

Oh, taste and see that the LORD is good.

PSALM 34:8

How girls were expected to behave

SPIRITUAL BEGINNINGS

The first person who told me about God

My first Communion

The first time I knew that God was real

Trust in the LORD with all your heart.

PROVERBS 3:5

Someone who helped me be as a Christian should

My Favorite Verse as a Child

The most wonderful thing about my father

My father was especially good at

My father let me "help" by

Lessons I learned from my father

The things my father taught me about God

Hear the instruction of your father.

PROVERBS 1:8

MY MOTHER'S KITCHEN

The most wonderful thing about my mother's kitchen

My mother let me "help" by

Lessons I learned from my mother

She watches over the ways of her household,
and does not eat the bread of idleness.

PROVERBS 31:27

My mother's best recipe

LESSONS IN LOVE
From My Mother

My mother's favorite piece of advice

_____

_____

_____

_____

_____

I never told my mother

_____

_____

_____

_____

What my mother taught me about God

_____

_____

_____

_____

_____

_____

_____

_____

My most memorable "woman-to-woman" talk with my mother

_____

_____

_____

_____

_____

_____

_____

_____

_____

She opens her mouth with wisdom,
and on her tongue is the law of kindness.

PROVERBS 31:26

EARLY SCHOOL YEARS

The school I attended

My favorite teacher and why

My best subject in school

A school event I will never forget

From childhood you have known the Holy Scriptures,
which are able to make you wise for salvation
through faith which is in Christ Jesus.

2 TIMOTHY 3:15

My best friend in elementary school

HIGH SCHOOL YEARS

The school I attended

My favorite teacher and why

The most important thing I learned

The friends I spent time with

Popular fads when I was in high school

Let no one despise your youth, but be an example to the believers
in word, in conduct, in love, in spirit, in faith, in purity.

1 TIMOTHY 4:12

MUSIC

Growing up, my favorite songs and musicians were

Now, I like to listen to

Your grandfather's and my favorite song

My favorite hymn

Sing to the LORD a new song.

PSALM 149:1

A song I want to share with you

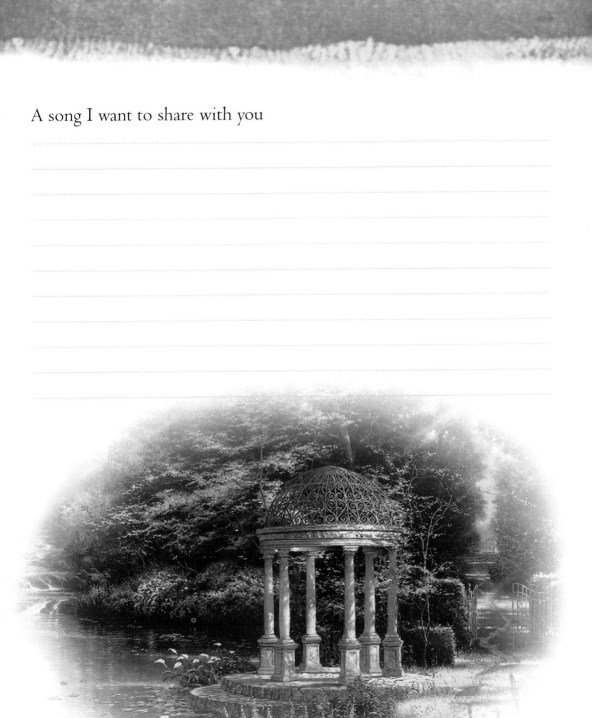

FIRST TIMES

The first time I drove a car

The first time I wore lipstick

The first time I voted in an election

My first real job

FRIENDSHIP

My best childhood friend

My best friend now

Being a good friend means

But there is a friend who sticks closer than a brother.

PROVERBS 18:24

Something I have learned about getting along with others

You are one of my best friends because

MY FIRST ROMANCE

My first "crush"

My first boyfriend

My first kiss

My first broken heart

My funniest experience on a date

And now abide faith, hope, love, these three;
but the greatest of these is love.

JOURNEYS

The first time I rode a bike

The best vacation we had as a family

My first plane trip

The LORD your God is with you wherever you go.

JOSHUA 1:9

The place I would most like to see

My most recent trip

SPIRITUAL LESSONS

I think faith is

_____

_____

_____

_____

_____

_____

A real Christian

_____

_____

_____

_____

My favorite passage of Scripture

God seems especially close when

Someone who helps me be a better Christian today

For God so loved the world that He gave His only
begotten Son, that whoever believes in Him should not
perish but have everlasting life.

JOHN 3:16

My Favorite Verse about Faith

GOALS

A goal I set and reached

My biggest disappointment

Defeat can be turned into success when

Let us lay aside every weight, and the sin which
so easily ensnares us, and let us run with endurance
the race that is set before us.

HEBREWS 12:1

A goal that I was proud to see you achieve

FALLING IN LOVE

I always thought that love was

God says that love is

How old I was and what I was doing when I met your grandfather

I was attracted to him because

Your grandfather proposed by

We love Him because He first loved us.

1 JOHN 4:19

MY WEDDING DAY

The day, time, and place we were married

What I wore

My attendants

What they wore

*Therefore a man shall leave his father and mother and be joined
to his wife, and they shall become one flesh.*

GENESIS 2:24

For our honeymoon, we went to

LIFE AS NEWLYWEDS

The first place we lived

Our first fight

One thing we still laugh about

Where we worship

Love never fails.

I CORINTHIANS 13:8

MY LIFE AS A MOTHER

Our children, their names and birth dates

The thing I love most about being a mother

The most difficult thing a mother has to do

My little children, let us not love in word
or in tongue, but in deed and in truth.

I JOHN 3:18

An important lesson I hope all my children and grandchildren learn

A PERSONAL FAITH

I know there is a God because

I experienced a turning point in my faith when

I have experienced God's clear guidance when

_____

_____

_____

_____

_____

_____

_____

_____

When I die, I believe that

_____

_____

_____

_____

_____

_____

_____

_____

_____

_____

Your word is a lamp to my feet and a light to my path.

PSALM 119:105

Thomas
Kinkade

My Favorite Verse about God

_____

_____

_____

_____

_____

_____

YOUR MOTHER

Your mother's full maiden name

_____

Her birthplace and date of birth

_____

The thing I love best about your mother

_____

_____

_____

_____

_____

_____

_____

_____

_____

_____

_____

Love one another fervently
with a pure heart.
I PETER 1:22

YOUR FATHER

Your father's full name

His birthplace and date of birth

The thing I love best about your father

YOU

When and where you were born

The first time I held you in my arms, I felt

The person in our family that you remind me of most

My Favorite Photo of You

I will praise You, for I am fearfully and wonderfully made;
marvelous are Your works, and that my soul knows very well.

PSALM 139:14

MY DREAMS FOR YOU

The ways you are like me

The ways you are different from me

One thing that I admire about you

Rejoice in the Lord always.
Again I will say, rejoice!

PHILIPPIANS 4:4

My prayer for you

CELEBRATING CHRISTMAS

My best Christmas ever

The real meaning of Christmas

Every Christmas, we

A favorite Christmas cookie recipe

For there is born to you this day in the city of David a Savior,
who is Christ the Lord.

LUKE 2:11

A FEW OF MY FAVORITE THINGS

My favorite books

My most comforting possession is

My most cherished piece of jewelry

For where your treasure is, there your heart will be also.

MATTHEW 6:21

That which I value most in life is

The dearest people on earth

The people I miss most

There is nothing more important than

In my life, I want to

For the LORD God is a sun and shield;
the LORD will give grace and glory.

PSALM 84:11

WINNING AT LIFE

I think that real success means

You are only a failure if

I believe that you could

All things are possible to him who believes.

MARK 9:23

I have seen you be a winner when

TIME WITH YOU

When we are together, I like to

One funny memory of you

I thank my God upon every remembrance of you.

PHILIPPIANS 1:3

One sweet memory of you

_____

_____

_____

_____

_____

_____

_____

_____

_____

_____

_____

_____

HOBBIES

My favorite hobby is

I would like to teach you to

Doing something you love is important because

Let all that you do be done with love.

1 CORINTHIANS 16:14

One thing we both love to do together

GROWING IN WISDOM

In my twenties, I thought I would

In my thirties, I became

In my forties, I wanted to

In my fifties, I discovered

Now that I am a grandmother

But the path of the just is like the shining sun,
that shines ever brighter unto the perfect day.

PROVERBS 4:18

SOMEDAY

When you have a grandchild, be sure to

Being a grandparent means

Never be too busy to

I have been young, and now am old; yet I have not seen the
righteous forsaken, nor his descendants begging bread.

PSALM 37:25

The best thing about being your grandmother

My Favorite Verse about Love

OUR FAMILY

Our Family Tree

Maternal Great-Grandmother

Date of Birth (death)

Maternal Great-Grandfather

Date of Birth (death)

Marriage

Paternal Great-Grandmother

Date of Birth (death)

Paternal Great-Grandfather

Date of Birth (death)

Marriage

Maternal Great-Grandmother

Date of Birth (death)

Maternal Great-Grandfather

Date of Birth (death)

Marriage

Paternal Great-Grandmother

Date of Birth (death)

Paternal Great-Grandfather

Date of Birth (death)

Marriage

Your Grandmother

Date of Birth (death)

Your Grandfather

Date of Birth (death)

Marriage

Your Grandmother

Date of Birth (death)

Your Grandfather

Date of Birth (death)

Marriage

Your Mother

Date of Birth (death)

Your Father

Date of Birth (death)

Marriage

You

Date of Birth

Your Sibling

Date of Birth

Your Sibling

Date of Birth

Your Sibling

Date of Birth

Your Sibling

Date of Birth

A Favorite Photo of You and Me

```
PLACE
A FAVORITE
PHOTO HERE
```

But as for me and my house, we will serve the LORD.

JOSHUA 24:15

INDEX OF PAINTINGS